BATON ROUGE

BATON ROUGE

Photographs and Text by

DAVID KING GLEASON

LOUISIANA STATE UNIVERSITY PRESS   BATON ROUGE

To Claudette, who inspired this project

Designer: Laura Roubique Gleason
Typeface: Janson Text
Typesetter: G & S Typesetters, Inc.
Printer and binder: Everbest Printing Co., Hong Kong, through
   Four Colour Imports, Ltd., Louisville, Kentucky

Library of Congress Cataloging-in-Publication Data

Gleason, David K.
    Baton Rouge : photographs and text / by David King Gleason.
        p.   cm.
    Includes index.
    ISBN 0-8071-1715-3
    1. Baton Rouge (La.)—Description.   2. Baton Rouge (La.)—
Description—Views.   I. Title.
F379.B33G57   1991
976.3'18—dc20   91-12477
                                             CIP

The paper in this book meets the guidelines for
permanence and durability of the Committee on
Production Guidelines for Book Longevity of the
Council on Library Resources. ∞

I am grateful to the many people who helped make this book a reality, including the good folks whom I know I'll inadvertently omit below because of my sometime memory.

Many thanks to Tom "Ed" McHugh, mayor of Baton Rouge, and Jim Brewer of the mayor's office; Fred Raiford of the Department of Public Works and Keith Roberson and Mike Monistere, the department's bucket truck operators; Everett Powers of the Arts Council of Greater Baton Rouge; Bob Hill of Springfield, Louisiana, who ferried me about the Tickfaw River; and Steve Verret, who showed me Spanish Lake.

I also appreciate the assistance of helicopter pilots John Blount, Ben Seal, and Tim Carbary and fixed-wing flier Mike Tillman; Bob Neese of the East Baton Rouge Parish School Board; Capt. Connie Swain of the LSU Campus Police and Gary Graham, director of Parking, Traffic, and Transportation at LSU; Karen St. Cyr of the Port Commission of Greater Baton Rouge; Carolyn Bennett and Alfred Ricard at Magnolia Mound plantation; Silvia Duke and Heywood Jeffers at the state senate; Mary Louise Prudhomme and Bob Riley at the Old State Capitol; Dale Emmanuel and Bonnie Schexnayder of Placid Refinery; Anne Wilkinson at Poplar Grove plantation; Mary Delle Gerald of the Cancer Society of Greater Baton Rouge; Vickie King of the Nature Conservancy; Rodney Lockett of Southern University Sports Information; Herb Vincent, Kent Lowe, Bill Franques, and Brad Messina of LSU Sports Information; Bud Courson of the Louisiana Department of Agriculture; Don Gerald and Lynn Brown of Ralph and Kacoo's Restaurant; Dan Lennie and helicopter pilot Jeff Brown of Acadian Ambulance Service; and Kathy Rossman, my long-suffering editor.

And countless thanks to my ever-lovin' wife Josie and our dedicated studio staff, who labored far beyond the call to bring this book to life. Gisela O'Brien made the reproduction-grade prints for *Baton Rouge*, Craig Saucier kept track of the innumerable negatives and prints and toted equipment, Cyndy Branton ran the front office, and Betty Brown kept the studio on an even keel. David Schlater volunteered much-appreciated help on some difficult interiors.

CONTENTS

DOWNTOWN

1 State Capitol
2 Pentagon Barracks
3 Old Arsenal
4 Governor's Mansion
5 Stewart-Dougherty House
6 Potts House
7 Saint Joseph's Cathedral
8 Saint James Episcopal Church
9 First Baptist Church
10 First United Methodist Church
11 First Presbyterian Church
12 Mount Zion First Baptist Church
13 Warden's House
14 Bogan Central Fire Station
15 Florence Coffeehouse
16 Tessier Buildings
17 LASC Riverside Museum
18 USS *Kidd* and Nautical Museum
19 Galvez Plaza
20 Old State Capitol
21 Lafayette Street Standpipe
22 City Club
23 Old Governor's Mansion
24 Saint Charles House (YWCO House)
25 Tabby's Blues Box and Heritage Hall

CITY AND SUBURBS

26 Magnolia Cemetery
27 Magnolia Mound
28 Louisiana State University
29 Louisiana School for the Deaf
30 Knox House
31 Manship House
32 Congregation B'Nai Israel
33 Baton Rouge General Medical Center
34 Goodwood
35 Mount Hope
36 Pennington Biomedical Research Center
37 Our Lady of the Lake Regional Medical Center
38 Jimmy Swaggart Ministries Complex
39 Bluebonnet Swamp
40 LSU Rural Life Museum
41 Spanish Lake
42 Joseph Kleinpeter House
43 Kleinpeter House
44 Santa Maria

45 Country Club of Louisiana
46 Baton Rouge Magnet High School
47 Scotlandville Magnet High School
48 Southern University
49 Scott's Bluff
50 Petrochemical plants
51 Port of Greater Baton Rouge
52 Greater Baton Rouge Zoo
53 Baton Rouge fairgrounds

THE ENVIRONS

54 The Diversion Canal and Blind River
55 Jefferson College
56 Oak Alley
57 Atchafalaya Swamp
58 Petrochemical plants
59 Nottoway
60 Brown Chapel Baptist Church
61 State Capitol Dragway
62 Old River Control Structure
63 Afton Villa gardens
64 Rosedown
65 Oakley

66 River Bend Nuclear Plant
67 Asphodel
68 Milbank
69 Glencoe
70 East Feliciana Parish Courthouse and Lawyers' Row
71 Linwood
72 Port Hudson battlefield
73 Poplar Grove

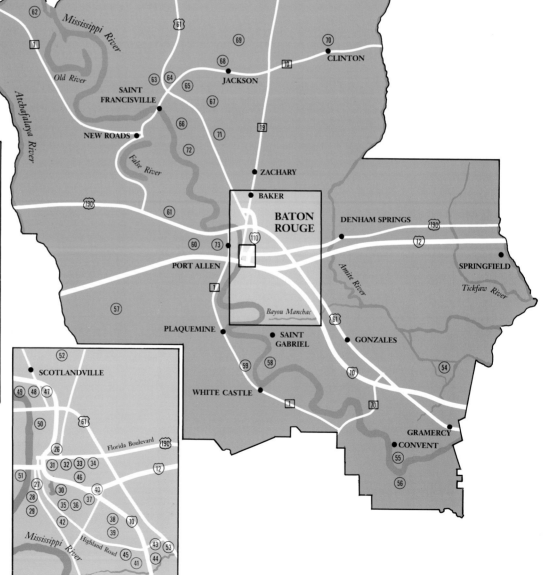

DOWNTOWN

CITY AND SUBURBS

Chet Boze

FOREWORD

WILLIAM R. BROCKWAY
Fellow, American Institute of Architects

Steeped in history and alive with change, Baton Rouge is a city that deserves to be better known than it is. The French term *baton rouge*, meaning "red stick," appears in the journals of the French explorer Pierre Le Moyne, Sieur d'Iberville, and his lieutenants in the year 1699. Ascending the Mississippi River, they noted the presence of a large, reddened pole, some 30 feet high, erected on a high bluff at an Indian encampment that was either 5 or 5½ leagues (the journals disagree) above Bayou Manchac on the right (east) side of the river. This *baton rouge* marked the boundary between the lands of the two major Indian tribes of the region, the Bayougoulas and the Oumas (Houmas). The exact spot where this totem once stood is not known today. "Baton Rouge" became the name of the settlement that grew up around the site.

Baton Rouge commands the first high ground to be found on the river, approximately one hundred miles north of the Gulf of Mexico. The city sits squarely astride the not-so-imaginary dividing line separating Anglo-American north Louisiana from the French-Spanish Creole development of the southern part of the state. As is common in such border communities, strong elements of both cultures can be found, even today, in the city's ethnic constituency and in its physical character.

The first Europeans to settle in the Baton Rouge area were French. Bernard Diron d'Artaguette, armed with a concession, or land grant, from the French Company of the Indies, began to develop a settlement at the site, probably in the year 1721. No physical evidence beyond a few yellowed documents in ancient European archives remains from this earliest attempt at colonization. Diron's little settlement apparently was not successful and seems to have either vanished or become moribund within a few years. But the later influx of British and Spanish settlers and military into the area after the 1763 partition of Louisiana, following the French and Indian Wars, resulted in viable communities being established at both Baton Rouge and Bayou Manchac.

Because of the town's strategic position between the expansionist territorial claims of the empire builders of Europe, who were jockeying for predominance in the New World, and because of its location on the principal waterway leading to the center of the continent, political control of the little community changed hands frequently. During the first 150 years of the town's existence, the flags of France, England, Spain, the inde-pendent republic of West Florida, the United States, and the Confederate States of America were flown over it, some of them more than once.

These and other influences have resulted in a rich and complex mixture of cultural, historic, military, political, and ethnic ingredients that give the city a flavor all its own. Long a magnet for historians and scholars, the city has in recent years seen the burgeoning of a young tourist industry; visitors are attracted by the many things to see and do in this unique community.

In Baton Rouge, centers of dynamic twentieth-century industrial development thrive alongside sleepy, oak-lined streets laid out in the eighteenth century. Buildings and other sites testify to the period of the area's colonization, the four battles fought within the city in three different wars, the period of occupation during the Civil War, Reconstruction, the tentative growth of the late nineteenth century, and the industrial expansion of today.

The economic base of Baton Rouge has changed dramatically over the years, as has that of much of the rest of the South, from agriculture to government, education, shipping, and industry. The city's Standard Oil refinery, the largest in the world when it was built in 1909, was the starting point of what is now a ninety-mile-long industrial corridor along the Mississippi River, stretching from Baton Rouge to New Orleans and beyond. Agricultural products, particularly soybeans and sugar, are still important contributors to the economy of the area, but have been outpaced by petroleum, chemicals, and nuclear power. The city's deep-water port is regularly ranked among the top four or five ports in the nation in terms of tonnage shipped.

Baton Rouge, the capital city of Louisiana, is home to the two largest universities in the state, Louisiana State University and Southern University. The magnet program within the public school system attracts some of the brightest students in the area. The city could boast of an established biracial commission long before the national civil rights movement of the 1960s.

Musical and theatrical events abound in Baton Rouge. In 1978, the city completed a $24 million cultural center, the Centroplex, to accommodate many of these activities. The Baton Rouge Symphony is recognized as one of the premier small-city orchestras in America and has performed at Carnegie Hall. The Baton Rouge Opera and LSU Opera Theater productions are well attended and have featured such world-class artists as Katherine

Luna, Martina Arroyo, and Jeffrey Wells. The Baton Rouge Ballet Theatre, the Baton Rouge Little Theater, and the Gilbert and Sullivan Society are equally impressive. For those interested in more earthy entertainment, the performances of Tabby's Blues Box, featuring both contemporary and traditional jazz and blues, are a must.

A yearly arts festival, known in Baton Rouge as FestForAll, attracts thousands of visitors from all over the country, who come to see and buy works by local artists and craftsmen, to sample Cajun and other ethnic cuisines, and to listen and dance to music of every stripe. The Cajun admonition to "pass a good time" is taken seriously in Baton Rouge.

The city strikes the visitor as a growing metropolitan complex that has not forgotten its small-town origins. Neighbors still take time to speak to one another, and school and church are important in the lives of many Baton Rougeans. In a recent listing of best places to live, Baton Rouge was rated among the top cities in the country.

A wide variety of impressive buildings, both old and new, can be found in Baton Rouge and its environs. In Baton Rouge there are two capitol buildings, and both are unique. In a country where so many state capitols are miniaturized versions of the Palladian, domed Capitol in Washington, D.C., both the Gothic Revival Old State Capitol, built in 1850 (which Mark Twain called a "little sham castle") and the present Art Deco skyscraper, built in 1932, are outstanding exceptions to the national norm.

There are also the Creole structures such as the Joseph Kleinpeter House, an early nineteenth-century cottage with hip roof, *bousillage* walls, and cypress floors. Another notable Creole structure is Magnolia Mound, built before 1800, with an umbrella roof, large window openings, raised floors, and a gallery all around—the eighteenth-century equivalent of modern passive solar design.

White-pillared, English-American mansion-style architecture, the type most often associated with the antebellum South, is common in the area and can be seen at its best in such buildings as Goodwood, Asphodel, Milbank, the Pentagon Barracks, and Manresa. Eastern classicism and later nineteenth-century eclectic styles appear in such buildings as the Stewart-Dougherty House, the Warden's House, and Rosedown. These styles culminate in the neo-Gothic Old State Capitol, the City Club, Saint James Episcopal Church, and Saint James's near neighbor Saint Joseph's Cathedral.

There is, however, much more than architectural variety in and around Baton Rouge for the weekend explorer to take in. There is the Greater Baton Rouge Zoo, the LSU Rural Life Museum, the USS *Kidd* and its companion nautical museum, False River, Nottoway plantation house. In season, there is baseball, basketball, and above all else, football at LSU and Southern University. A few miles west of the city is one of the finest drag-racing tracks in the country, attracting national competitors. Mardi Gras is celebrated with parades and revelry in many parts of the city and a number of surrounding communities. The annual Greater Baton Rouge State Fair, the Great River Road Run, and fishing, boating, and water skiing in nearby waterways all provide unequaled recreation possibilities for visitor and resident alike.

David King Gleason is an artist in love with his subject, and it shows in his work. For more than thirty years, he has chronicled the historic architecture of many parts of the nation and the lower Mississippi valley in particular, with numerous beautifully illustrated books and portfolios to his credit. In this volume, Gleason's talents have been brought to bear on a wide range of subject matter. Through the medium of color photography, he provides the reader with a series of tantalizing vignettes of the historic and cultural melange that is Baton Rouge. From dramatic views of the city's present-day skyline to primeval scenes in the Bluebonnet and Atchafalaya swamps, from evocative portraits of antebellum architectural grandeur to a picturesque glimpse of an old, weathered church near a former sugar plantation—not to mention pictures of Cajun cooking, industrial plants, festivals, cemeteries, battlegrounds, and dozens of other scenes—he portrays for us the sights and sounds and tastes of this most unusual city in all its wondrous diversity.

Read and enjoy.

PART I
DOWNTOWN AND THE SUBURBS

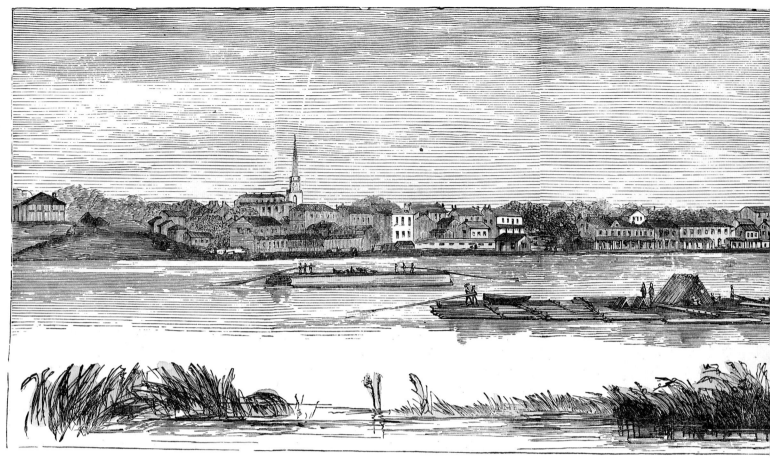

BATON ROUGE, 1864

In a Civil War view featured in *Harper's Weekly*, Baton Rouge was an occupied city, governed by northern generals until the end of Reconstruction in 1877. The Gothic State Capitol building, a billet for Union troops, stands at the right of this view; the five-story State School for the Deaf and Dumb is at the extreme right. Saint Joseph's Cathedral, begun in 1830, is at the left.

BATON ROUGE, 1990

In a twilight view of the Baton Rouge skyline in the spring of 1990, the 1932 State Capitol building is at the left. Reflecting the last rays of the sunset is One American Place, now the headquarters of Hancock Bank of Louisiana. To the right of One American Place is the spire of Saint Joseph's Cathedral. At the center are the two towers of Premier Bank. The Old State Capitol is toward the right, and next to it are the larger Municipal Building and the Centroplex municipal auditorium.

BATON ROUGE PANORAMA, 1912

During the spring of 1912, Baton Rouge photographer Jasper Ewing lugged a large panoramic camera up the mast of the USS *Nebraska* for an overall view of his adopted town. The spire of Saint Joseph's Cathedral is recognizable at the center left, and the Old State Capitol is at the right.

Louisiana and Lower Mississippi Valley Collections, Louisiana State University Libraries

Baton Rouge, 1990

DOWNTOWN BATON ROUGE, 1924

This early aerial view looking northeast across the State Capitol predates the construction of many of today's downtown "landmarks." At the left is the water tower of the Baton Rouge Water Company. Running diagonally across the upper right of the picture is Fourth Street (Church Street), still home to Saint James Episcopal Church, on the corner of Convention and Church streets. Proceeding northward from Saint James in 1924 were the Presbyterian Church of Baton Rouge, Saint Joseph's Academy, and the Methodist Episcopal Church of Baton Rouge. Saint Joseph's Cathedral is just out of the picture at the top center.

DOWNTOWN BATON ROUGE, 1990

Clockwise from the Old State Capitol in this view are the red brick Saint James Episcopal Church at about 12:00, the City Club (the post office in 1924) at about 1:00, and the downtown library and the Municipal Building at about 2:00. A corner of the Centroplex auditorium is at 4:30, and at 7:00 is the Louisiana Arts and Science Center, formerly the Illinois Central railroad station. The water tower is at 9:00, along with the old Heidelberg Hotel. At about 10:00 are the glass-covered One American Place, the State Natural Resources Building, and Saint Joseph's Cathedral. The two towers of Premier Bank are at about 11:00.

OLD STATE CAPITOL

After Louisiana's 1845 constitutional convention mandated a move from New Orleans, Baton Rouge was selected to become the site of the new capitol of the Pelican State. James Dakin, a New York architect who had recently moved to New Orleans, prepared plans for a neo-Gothic castle overlooking the Mississippi River. Completed in 1849 at a cost of $396,000, the statehouse was gutted by a fire started (perhaps accidentally) by Union troops in 1862.

The building once again became Louisiana's

capitol after it was rebuilt by architect William Freret in 1882. Freret added another floor and a cast-iron spiral staircase. The central rotunda at the top of the stairs provides access to governmental offices and to the Senate and House chambers. It is dramatically illuminated by a stained-glass dome supported by a tapering, cast-iron center column.

HOUSE CHAMBER, OLD STATE CAPITOL

In this room on January 26, 1861, a Louisiana convention approved an ordinance of secession that removed the state from the Union and formed an independent republic. Two months later, Louisiana joined the Confederacy. Less than two years later, on December 28, 1862, the interior of the Old State Capitol lay in ashes. It was rebuilt later. Huey Long was the last to govern Louisiana from executive offices in the Old State Capitol.

The state legislature held its opening meeting in the Old State Capitol for the first time in nearly fifty years in the spring of 1990. After a short meeting in its smaller chamber (shown next page), the Senate repaired to the House chamber to hear an address by Governor Buddy Roemer to the joint session of the legislature.

SENATE CHAMBER, OLD STATE CAPITOL

In May of 1929, the Senate of the state of Louisiana convened in this room as a court of impeachment against then-governor Huey Long (he was not convicted).

THIRD STREET

Once the capital city's centerpiece of commercial activity, Third Street (which runs north
and south, paralleling the river) reached its
height of retail development in the late 1950s.
Downtown today has become Baton Rouge's
major financial and government district, as re-
tailing has moved to the shopping centers and
boulevards of the south and east.

At the left is Third Street in 1959, in this
view looking north from the existing base of
the Confederate statue on North Boulevard.
Above is Third Street during the 1990 Fest-
ForAll, photographed from a bucket truck
positioned next to the monument.

PENTAGON BARRACKS

In 1819, Lt. Col. Zachary Taylor began supervising the construction of the Pentagon Barracks on high ground overlooking the Mississippi River north of present downtown Baton Rouge. The barracks were to house a regiment of infantry troops, needed because the young state of Louisiana bordered the Spanish territory of Texas. Taylor settled in Baton Rouge, achieved fame as "Old Rough and Ready" during the Mexican War in 1845, and was elected president of the United States in 1848.

The two-story buildings (there are four—the open side of the pentagon faces the Mississippi) currently include a visitor center for the State Capitol complex and apartments for state legislators.

OLD ARSENAL

The Pentagon Barracks became part of an eleven-building ordnance complex occupying much of what is now the grounds of the State Capitol. On the eastern end (at the left) remains the Old Arsenal, with walls four and one-half feet thick, built in 1838 as a powder magazine.

Headquarters for Union troops during the Civil War, the complex became the campus of Louisiana State University in 1886. In 1925, the campus moved south of downtown Baton Rouge. The school, originally called the Seminary of Learning of the State of Louisiana, had moved from central Louisiana to Baton Rouge after an 1869 fire and had merged with the State Agricultural and Mechanical College, formerly located in New Orleans, in 1877.

STATE CAPITOL BUILDING

The present State Capitol building was the brainchild of former governor Huey Long, who saw his dream of the tallest state capitol in the continental United States become a reality when it was dedicated in the spring of 1932, after only fourteen months of construction. Believing that the Old State Capitol (where he was impeached) was obsolete, Long had lobbied the legislature for $5 million in construction funds, stating that a large building housing all the state agencies would pay for itself in efficiency.

Long's magnificent 34-story Art Deco skyscraper stands 450 feet tall. Long was assassinated there in 1935.

MEMORIAL HALL,
STATE CAPITOL

The great room of the statehouse is the lavishly ornamented Memorial Hall, 124 feet long and 40 feet wide, with a 37-foot ceiling. A bronze relief map of the Pelican State is in the center; bronze elevator doors with portraits of all the state's governors through Huey Long are at the right. At either end of the hall are bronze doors to the House and Senate chambers.

The House Chamber

The Senate Chamber

A View of the Capitol Grounds from the Top of the State Capitol

GOVERNOR'S MANSION

Built under the administration of former governor Jimmie Davis, this stately 40-room executive mansion was patterned after the classic Oak Alley plantation home. Completed in 1963, the Greek Revival house, with 12 bedrooms and 16 baths, was designed by Shreveport architect William C. Gilmer. It replaced the earlier mansion built by Huey Long on North Boulevard.

STEWART-DOUGHERTY HOUSE
left

Used as a Union hospital in 1862 and 1863, the Stewart-Dougherty House, located on North Street in downtown Baton Rouge, has remained in the same family since its construction in the 1840s. It has always been inherited by a woman. The family's plantation acreage is to the north of town.

The four square columns in the front of the two-story house are of plaster over brick. The railing is iron, as is the original fence.

POTTS HOUSE

Nelson Potts, master brick mason, moved from New Jersey to Baton Rouge in the middle 1840s and built his own home on North Street as a showpiece for his work in 1846. Located in Spanish Town, a few blocks from the Stewart-Dougherty House (which he also built), the house has eight rooms—four upstairs and four downstairs—plus a center hall. Two years after the Civil War, with the local economy shattered, Potts returned to New Jersey.

DOWNTOWN CHURCHES

Fourth Street was once home to most of Baton Rouge's churches, but as the city expanded, so did the congregations, which built new sanctuaries across East Baton Rouge Parish. In many American cities, downtown congregations have lost a major part of their membership to the suburbs, but in Louisiana's capital city, downtown churches are active and prosperous.

In this aerial photograph, looking northwest, First United Methodist Church is in the lower left corner, at the intersection of Interstate 110 (to the east) and North Boulevard. Also on North Boulevard (toward the west), on the side of the street opposite the Methodist church, is First Presbyterian Church. On Convention Street, which runs parallel to North Boulevard, is the white-columned First Baptist Church and the red brick Gothic Revival Saint James Episcopal Church, at the in-tersection of Convention and Fourth streets. In the upper right corner is the steeple of Saint Joseph's Cathedral, located at the corner of Fourth and Main streets.

SAINT JOSEPH'S CATHEDRAL

The first Catholic church in Baton Rouge, the Church of Our Lady of Sorrows, was built before 1792 on land believed to be north of the present State Capitol. When Father Charles Burke, an Irish priest who had studied in Spain, arrived in Baton Rouge, one of his first acts was to perform the marriage of Don Antonio de Gras and Genevieve Dulat there.

Don Antonio donated land on the present site of Saint Joseph's for a new sanctuary, which was built in the late 1790s. The present structure, completed in 1853, was damaged by Union gunboats during the Battle of Baton Rouge. It became a cathedral in 1961 with the installation of Robert E. Tracy as the first bishop of the Diocese of Baton Rouge.

SAINT JAMES EPISCOPAL CHURCH *left*

Although Episcopalians held their first services in Baton Rouge in 1819, the congregation of Saint James Episcopal Church was not chartered until 1844. Mrs. Zachary Taylor, wife of General Taylor, was one of the founders. The parish began construction of its first sanctuary the following year. The present Gothic Revival building was completed in 1895 and is distinguished by its three Tiffany stained-glass windows over the altar.

FIRST BAPTIST CHURCH

The Baptist heritage in Baton Rouge began with the formation of the city's first Baptist congregation in 1838. Continuing that tradition, the congregation of First Baptist Church was organized in 1874. Beginning with eighteen members, this Baptist church is now one of the largest in Louisiana. The present, white-columned building was completed in 1955 and is the fourth home for the First Baptist congregation in Baton Rouge.

The pageant shown here, the Greater Baton Rouge Christmas Celebration, is presented annually by the church's one-hundred-member sanctuary choir and thirty-piece orchestra.

MOUNT ZION FIRST BAPTIST CHURCH

The Gothic-style sanctuary of Mount Zion
First Baptist Church, located at 356 East Bou-
levard, was designed by Baton Rouge architect
A. Hays Town and was dedicated in 1952. One
of the largest Baptist churches serving the
black community of Baton Rouge, Mount
Zion has had the same pastor, the Reverend
T. J. Jemison, since the building's construction.
   Mount Zion's adult choir, shown here, is
one of the city's best-known vocal groups.

WARDEN'S HOUSE

Antebellum Baton Rouge was the location of the Louisiana Penitentiary, situated on a tract of land bordered by Florida and Laurel streets, between Seventh and Twelfth streets. Across Laurel stood the home of the warden, a two-story Georgian brick building completed in 1839. The warden's quarters were upstairs, and a store that sold prisoner-made articles was downstairs. The smaller kitchen wing can be seen to the right.

The penitentiary has long since moved to West Feliciana Parish, north of Baton Rouge, but the Warden's House remains. The building was restored in 1967.

BOGAN CENTRAL FIRE STATION

Located in the 400 block of Laurel Street is the Bogan Central Fire Station, built in 1924. It now houses a firefighters' museum on the first floor and the offices of the Arts Council of Greater Baton Rouge on the second floor. It is listed on the National Register of Historic Places.

FLORENCE COFFEEHOUSE

In the 100 block of Main Street, Nelson Potts, master brick mason, built a commercial-residential townhouse for Johan and Lucas Florence in 1850. The handmade red brick probably came from Potts's own brickyard, near the intersection of Ninth Street and Spanish Town Road.

A coffeehouse (saloon) was located on the first floor, which was later raised nearly three feet to avoid flooding from the Mississippi River. At the rear of the building is a small patio. Living quarters were originally on the second floor.

The building underwent a succession of owners and was altered for a series of different commercial enterprises over the next 120 years. The Florence Coffeehouse was given an adaptive restoration in 1971.

TESSIER BUILDINGS

Overlooking the Mississippi River in the 300 block of Lafayette Street, just north of the Capitol House Hotel, are three of the oldest buildings in Baton Rouge: the Tessier Buildings, *ca.* 1800. These structures were named after their builder, Charles R. Tessier, who extended an official welcome on behalf of Baton Rouge to the marquis de Lafayette when he visited the town in 1825.

GALVEZ PLAZA

Between the Centroplex branch of the East
Baton Rouge Parish Library System and the
Old State Capitol is the Marcha de Gálvez,
Galvez Plaza. The plaza commemorates the
1779 victory of Spanish forces over the British
who occupied Baton Rouge and West Florida
at the time.

   Dominating the plaza is a bronze sculpture
by Frank Hayden of Oliver Pollock, aide-de-
camp to Spanish governor Bernardo de Gálvez, commander of the Spanish and American
forces. Pollock represented the Continental
Congress to the Spanish government, and it is
widely believed that the dollar sign ($) origi-
nated with him.

LASC RIVERSIDE MUSEUM

In 1925, the Yazoo and Mississippi Valley Railroad built its first passenger station in Baton Rouge, facing the Old State Capitol and situated along tracks paralleling the Mississippi River. The Illinois Central system later acquired the line and then leased the station to the Louisiana Arts and Science Center in 1971 after it discontinued passenger service.

Now the LASC Riverside Museum, the complex includes a steam-driven passenger train complete with a restored diner and coaches, an art gallery, river overlooks, and a children's Discovery Depot.

LAFAYETTE STREET STANDPIPE

Built of cast iron in 1888, the Lafayette Street Standpipe is 100 feet tall and held 145,000 gallons of water when it was in service from 1888 until its retirement in 1963. Listed on the National Register of Historic Places, the tower was designated a national landmark by the American Water Works Association in 1990.

In the background is the Capitol House Hotel, originally the Heidelberg, located only a block away from the Old State Capitol and once frequented by Huey Long. The hotel is also on the National Register.

USS *KIDD* AND NAUTICAL MUSEUM

Resting in a unique cradle that allows it to float during high water on the Mississippi River, the USS *Kidd*, an authentically restored 2,050-ton Fletcher-class World War II destroyer, was brought to Baton Rouge in 1982 and opened to the public the following year. In the ensuing seven years, 60 tons of World War II equipment were added, including 20-mm and 40-mm guns, torpedo tubes, depth charges, and radar. A silver service graces the officers' wardroom.

The *Kidd* earned four battle stars in the Pacific theater and survived a kamikaze hit in April, 1945. It was mothballed in 1964.

Across the levee from the *Kidd* is a nautical history museum, designed by Desmond and Associates, architects, and opened in 1987.

Nautical Museum

CITY CLUB AND WCTU STATUE

Looking south on North Boulevard is the privately owned City Club of Baton Rouge. The Renaissance Revival building with its extensive terra-cotta ornamentation served as Baton Rouge's post office from 1895, the year it was built, until 1933, when it became the city hall. Baton Rouge completed the new, larger Municipal Building in 1956 and leased the old post office to the City Club in 1957.

In the middle ground of North Boulevard, in front of the City Club, stands a bronze statue of Hebe, daughter of Zeus and Hera, who is best known in Greek mythology as the cupbearer (wine bearer) to the gods. The statue was presented to the city of Baton Rouge in 1914 by the Women's Christian Temperance Union.

OLD GOVERNOR'S MANSION

In addition to authorizing the building of the present State Capitol, Huey Long was responsible for the construction on North Boulevard of what is now called the Old Governor's Mansion. It replaced an antebellum home bought by the state in 1887 to house its chief executive. Completed in 1930, the Georgian Revival mansion was home to Louisiana's governors for thirty years, until Jimmie Davis, governor from 1944 to 1948 and from 1960 to 1964, had a new official residence built near the present capitol.

On the National Register of Historic Places, the mansion is now restored to the 1930s. Its major rooms and bedrooms contain furniture and memorabilia of the governors who resided there.

SAINT CHARLES HOUSE
(YWCO HOUSE) *right*

One of the larger homes in Beauregard Town, Saint Charles House was built around the turn of the century for J. K. Romaine, the city's leading jeweler. After an expansion of the house in the 1940s by architect A. Hays Town, the Romaine family donated it to the Young Women's Christian Association in the 1950s. In a 1960s reorganization, ownership of the house was transferred to a local nonprofit group, the Young Women's Christian Organization. Listed on the National Register of Historic Places, this Victorian house is well maintained by the YWCO as a landmark of Beauregard Town.

BEAUREGARD TOWN

About 1805, when Baton Rouge was part of Spanish West Florida, Elias Beauregard commissioned Arsene LaCarriere LaTour to lay out a new subdivision for the settlement, which he envisioned as becoming the major part of the town. Development of the area, bordered by North, South, and East boulevards and the Mississippi River was relatively slow, but stable. Now a historic district, Beauregard Town has a large number of relatively unchanged, middle-class, late nineteenth- and early twentieth-century houses, exemplified by the homes in this view of the 200 block of Napoleon Street.

MAGNOLIA MOUND

On high ground overlooking the floodplain of the Mississippi River, south of downtown Baton Rouge, is one of Louisiana's oldest wooden structures, Magnolia Mound plantation house. Built about 1791, it has been restored to the period of the early 1800s by the Foundation for Historical Louisiana and the East Baton Rouge Parish Recreation and Park Commission. Listed on the National Register of Historic Places, Magnolia Mound was the manor house of a 900-acre plantation, whose crops included indigo, cotton, and sugarcane. Thanks to the efforts of a highly professional staff and a large number of volunteers, Magnolia Mound successfully re-creates the atmosphere of life on an early nineteenth-century Louisiana plantation.

The parlor at Magnolia Mound has a handsome cove ceiling, probably installed in the early 1800s at the direction of Armand and Constance Duplantier, who also added the dining room at the rear.

The kitchen was rebuilt in 1979 on the foundations of the original cookhouse, separate from the main house because of the ever-present danger of fire. Docents cook weekly, using the methods, recipes, and utensils of the early 1800s.

In another outbuilding, a restored pigeonnier to the rear of Magnolia Mound, schoolchildren learn early nineteenth-century techniques of weaving.

Magnolia Mound

LOUISIANA STATE UNIVERSITY

The institution that is known today as Louisiana State University was established in Pineville, Louisiana, in 1860. Its first superintendent, of less than a year, was William Tecumseh Sherman, who resigned to acquire fame as one of the Union's great Civil War generals. The Baton Rouge campus was first situated on the northern side of town, in the former arsenal complex. The complex had been the site of military installations since the late 1700s. Between 1925 and 1930, the campus was gradually moved south of town to the 650-acre Gartness plantation, just below Magnolia Mound. Dedicated in 1926, the Baton Rouge campus contains more than 250 principal buildings. The current student body numbers over 26,000.

In this aerial view looking northwest across LSU, the campus is in the foreground and downtown Baton Rouge is at the upper right, with the Interstate 10 bridge crossing the Mississippi River.

PARADE GROUND AND MEMORIAL TOWER

Part of the original LSU campus on the present site, Memorial Tower was dedicated to LSU students who died in World War II. Housed within the tower is the Anglo-American Art Museum, featuring a permanent fine arts collection and period re-creations of rooms from American and British homes. In front of the tower lies the parade ground, where intramural sporting events often take place.

Indian Mounds on the LSU campus overlook the floodplain of the Mississippi River. Mound Builders inhabited the Baton Rouge area at about the time of Julius Caesar.

FRENCH HOUSE

The French House was constructed in 1935 in the style of a French château. In a unique LSU program, students of Romance languages, both male and female, lived in the building, studied the French language, literature, and history, and experienced French cuisine. The château became a conventional dormitory in 1958 and in 1979 and 1980 was restored to provide office space.

LSU QUADRANGLE

In this view looking north across the quadrangle, downtown Baton Rouge is at the top of the picture. At the right are the LSU Student Union and parade ground. The quadrangle is bounded on three sides by the original classroom buildings of the Baton Rouge campus. Their red tile rooftops echo the Mediterranean look of the early campus in the 1920s. At the top end of the quadrangle is the newer Troy H. Middleton Library. Outside the quadrangle, at the lower right, is the Howe-Russell Geoscience Complex, and the flat-topped School of Design is at the lower left.

Sorority Row at LSU

LOUISIANA SCHOOL FOR THE DEAF

In 1858, Louisiana established a state school for the deaf, mute, and blind in Baton Rouge. The school was located in Beauregard Town in a building bordered by Saint Ferdinand and Mayflower streets and South Boulevard. When the school later split into two separate institutions, the school for the deaf remained at the Beauregard Town location until 1977, when it moved to its present 115-acre campus, designed by New Orleans architect Humberto Fontave, on Brightside Drive, south of LSU.

The Louisiana School for the Deaf has a student enrollment of 450 in resident and outreach programs, spanning ages from birth to twenty-one.

KNOX HOUSE *left*

When first built, this neo–Greek Revival mansion, situated on its own peninsula on City Park Lake, was known as the Knox House.

MANSHIP HOUSE

Built in 1928 in Baton Rouge's Garden District, the Manship House is listed on the National Register of Historic Places. Lewis Gross was the architect of this Renaissance Revival house, built for Charles Manship, publisher of Baton Rouge's *State-Times* and *Morning Advocate* newspapers.

GARDEN DISTRICT

The oldest part of the Garden District is the Roseland Terrace subdivision, site of the Baton Rouge Racetrack around the turn of the century. Homes in the 2300 block of Myrtle Street (shown here) are typical of the Garden District. Other early homes in Roseland Terrace were built in 1911.

CONGREGATION B'NAI ISRAEL

In 1858, when Baton Rouge was only a town,
the Hebrew Congregation of Baton Rouge was
formed. After the Civil War, the congregation
worshiped at Dalsheimer Hall until it pur-
chased a former Catholic Brothers' school at
Fifth and Laurel streets in March, 1887. Today it is known as the Congregation B'Nai
Israel. The present temple, shown here during
a wedding ceremony, was built in 1954 in the
3300 block of Kleinert Avenue, east of the
Garden District. The temple is distinguished
by its growing collection of religious art.

SAINT JOSEPH'S ALTAR AT OUR LADY OF MERCY CATHOLIC CHURCH

Preserving a venerated custom from Palermo, Sicily, the Grandsons of Italy build an altar honoring Saint Joseph on the weekend nearest Saint Joseph's Day, March 19, at Our Lady of Mercy Catholic Church in Baton Rouge. Volunteers begin cooking and baking dishes for the altar in January. The lavish spread includes Italian bread, cookies, and cakes, and fruits, vegetables, and wine (no meat is present at a Saint Joseph's Altar).

At the table in the foreground, those portraying Joseph (Giuseppe), Mary, and Jesus are served first to begin the 11:00 A.M. Sunday feast.

MAGNOLIA CEMETERY *right*

In the foreground is Magnolia Cemetery, established out in the country, east of what was then Baton Rouge, before the Civil War. In this view looking westward toward downtown Baton Rouge, Florida Boulevard is at the left, then Laurel, Main, and North streets. Across the top third of the photograph is the expressway, I-110, at approximately the eastern limits of pre–Civil War Baton Rouge. In the middle ground, between Laurel and Main streets, is the downtown location of Maison Blanche, formerly Goudchaux's department store.

In August, 1862, Confederate troops approached Baton Rouge from the east in an abortive effort to drive out Union forces occupying the capital city. The heaviest fighting ranged in and around Magnolia Cemetery and reached as far west as the other side of the present expressway. Approximately 5,000 troops were involved. Many of the over 800 casualties are buried in Magnolia Cemetery and across Florida Boulevard in the Federal Cemetery, which was established after the battle.

Magnolia Cemetery

BATON ROUGE GENERAL MEDICAL CENTER

The roots of Baton Rouge General Medical Center go back to a clinic on the corner of Church (now Fourth) Street and Florida Boulevard, begun by Dr. T. P. Singletary in 1908. In 1924, women of the Charity Ward Association, which had assumed financial responsibility for the establishment, raised $150,000 for a new, 64-bed hospital at East Boulevard and Government Street.

In 1944, planning began for another, larger hospital building (on the present site, at Florida Boulevard and Acadian Throughway), and in 1950, the move to the new, 250-bed hospital was completed.

Now the flagship of the General Health System, Baton Rouge General Medical Center has expanded to become a highly sophisticated, 450-bed, not-for-profit hospital.

MOUNT HOPE

One of Baton Rouge's antebellum showplaces is Mount Hope, located on Highland Road in the Dutch Highlands. This area was settled by Pennsylvania German farmers in the 1790s, south of the original town. Mount Hope was built in 1817 by Joseph Sharp, who had acquired a 400-acre Spanish land grant in 1786. Sharp was one of the leaders of the Florida Rebellion that ended Spanish domination in 1810.

Restored in the late 1970s, the house is now open to the public.

PENNINGTON BIOMEDICAL RESEARCH CENTER

C. B. "Doc" Pennington donated over $125 million to establish the Pennington Biomedical Research Center, which is part of the LSU system. The sophisticated complex covers an area the size of five football fields. Scientists at the center are engaged in a wide range of research in, for example, molecular nutrition, the correlation between serum cholesterol and heart attacks, and the effect of diet on mental performance.

OUR LADY OF THE LAKE
REGIONAL MEDICAL CENTER

Originally established just north of the Old
State Capitol in downtown Baton Rouge, Our
Lady of the Lake Hospital began serving the
capital city in 1923. The hospital moved to a
new complex on Essen Lane in 1978 and is
now known as Our Lady of the Lake Regional
Medical Center.

JIMMY SWAGGART MINISTRIES COMPLEX

Constructed in the 1980s, the Jimmy Swaggart Ministries complex is located on both sides of Bluebonnet Boulevard near Interstate 10. The 270-acre facility includes a Bible college, which opened in 1984, a printing and mailing center, a recording studio, and a television production studio.

BLUEBONNET SWAMP

Curving across the lower end of Bluebonnet Boulevard, near its intersection with Highland Road, is a pristine, old-growth, cypress-tupelo-maple swamp, the 70-acre Bluebonnet Swamp. Some of its trees are more than two hundred years old.

The Louisiana Nature Conservancy recently negotiated a purchase of a portion of the swamp to preserve this unique natural wetland for future generations.

LSU RURAL LIFE MUSEUM

This remarkable complex of restored nine-teenth-century dwellings includes a sugar-house, slave cabins, an overseer's house, a barn, and farming equipment. It was assembled by landscape architect Steele Burden, who began collecting early-Louisiana rural structures and implements after World War II.

Located off Interstate 12 near Essen Lane, the LSU Rural Life Museum is considered one of the best small museums in the country. Also at the site is the LSU rose garden.

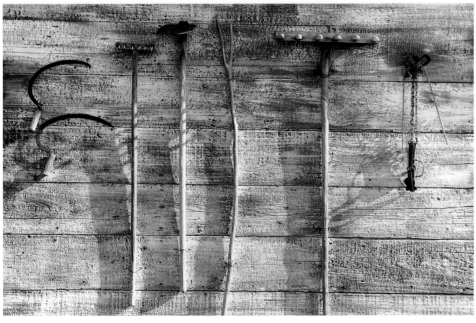

SPANISH LAKE

Just below Bayou Manchac, the southern
boundary of East Baton Rouge Parish, is
Spanish Lake, so-named for the Spaniards who
settled nearby at the intersection of Bayou
Manchac and the Mississippi River. They later
moved to Spanish Town in Baton Rouge, near
the present State Capitol. The natural lake and
adjacent cypress swamp—where eagles nest—
are accessible by canoe from Alligator Bayou,
which connects the lake with Bayou Manchac.

JOSEPH KLEINPETER HOUSE
(on Highland Road)

An early nineteenth-century Creole cottage, the Joseph Kleinpeter House was rescued from probable demolition by Baton Rouge attorney Robert Hodges. Hodges moved the house to a compatible location on Highland Road and gave it an exhaustive and painstaking restoration.

Hodges reconstructed the original hip roof, removing gables added later, and, after much experimentation, rebuilt the *bousillage* (plaster over mud and moss) walls. He also uncovered the original cypress floors and reconstructed the windows and doors to their original configuration.

The project won the 1989 grand prize of the Great American Home Awards, sponsored by the National Trust for Historic Preservation.

KLEINPETER HOUSE
(on Perkins Road)

Still standing on part of its plantation acreage, though moved from its original site in the middle 1980s, is the Kleinpeter House. Construction dates of the house range from twenty years before the Civil War to after the war. Nominated for inclusion on the National Register of Historic Places, the Kleinpeter House is considered "a rare surviving example of a Greek Revival cottage within the context of East Baton Rouge Parish." Always a part of the Kleinpeter family property (the family moved into this area in the 1790s), it was restored by Benjamin Kleinpeter in the late 1980s.

SANTA MARIA

Built in the 1870s for Charles Knowlton, a
Civil War captain in the Tenth Louisiana Infantry, Santa Maria is the only raised Greek
Revival cottage in East Baton Rouge Parish
and the only remaining plantation house with
a full complement of outbuildings. The 740-
acre plantation's major crops were first sugarcane and then cotton. Knowlton sold Santa
Maria in 1901.

COUNTRY CLUB OF LOUISIANA

Opened in 1986, the Country Club of Louisiana is built around an 18-hole golf course, designed by Jack Nicklaus and rated number one in Louisiana by *Golf Digest* magazine. The club has 750 members.

Beginning about 500 B.C., Indians inhabited the 844 acres near the intersection of bayous Manchac and Fountain where the Country Club is now located. The explorer Pierre Le Moyne, Sieur d'Iberville passed the site in 1699 on his first trip to Louisiana. Later the land became part of the Kleinpeter family acreage.

GOODWOOD

Goodwood plantation once covered extensive acreage east of Baton Rouge, reaching beyond what is now Airline Highway, with the current Goodwood subdivision at its center. Facing Goodwood Avenue is the white-columned Goodwood mansion, built for Dr. S. G. Laycock in 1856. Dr. Laycock had his own racetrack near Jefferson Highway, the Goodwood Racetrack.

The two-story brick house, with 14-foot ceilings downstairs, was built with running water piped to washstands in each bedroom, and it still has its original heart-pine flooring and marble fireplaces. The original kitchen building is to the rear of the house, at the left in this photograph.

BATON ROUGE MAGNET HIGH SCHOOL

Built in 1926, this three-story building on Government Street is the second site of Baton Rouge High School, which was previously located downtown. Now a college-preparatory magnet school, Baton Rouge High draws students from across East Baton Rouge Parish.

Baton Rouge High is known for its excellence in academics and visual and performing arts as well as for its student-run radio station, WBRH. The school was one of the first in the nation honored by the Presidential Commission on Excellence in Education.

SCOTLANDVILLE MAGNET HIGH SCHOOL *below*

Scotlandville High School was named a magnet school in 1982. With its "magnet within a magnet" program, Scotlandville High draws pupils preparing for the engineering professions from across East Baton Rouge Parish, as well as college-preparatory students from the northern half of the parish. Of its over 1,000 students, 98 percent go on to college. Scotlandville High has been nominated by the State Department of Education as a "high school of distinction" in the national School of Excellence program.

SOUTHERN UNIVERSITY

The nation's largest predominately black university, Southern University has a 600-acre main campus situated on a bluff at a great westward bend in the Mississippi River north of Baton Rouge. It is possible that the red pole (*baton rouge* in French) seen by Pierre Le Moyne, Sieur d'Iberville, on his trip through the area in 1699 overlooked the river from Scott's Bluff, the high ground on which the campus is located.

Southern opened its doors in New Orleans to twelve students in 1881 and then moved to Baton Rouge in 1914. Presently, there are

more than 8,500 students enrolled at Southern's Baton Rouge campus. The school also has branch campuses in New Orleans and Shreveport.

In this view looking east toward the campus of Southern University, Scott's Bluff is in the foreground.

A memorial sculpture of the red stick that gave Baton Rouge its name stands on Scott's Bluff. The monument was fashioned by one of the state's preeminent sculptors, Frank Hayden, a member of Southern University's faculty until his death in 1988.

The John B. Cade Library (at left) and the Smith-Brown Memorial Student Union building overlook Lake Kernan, on the Southern University campus.

Shown here is a rehearsal of Southern's Jazz Ensemble, a nationally known instrumental and vocal group directed by Alvin Batiste.

At Scott's Bluff, the Mississippi makes a great turn
toward the west. The Southern football stadium,
home of the Jaguars, is in the foreground.

PORT OF GREATER BATON ROUGE

At the head of deep-water navigation on the Mississippi River is the Port of Greater Baton Rouge, the nation's fifth-largest port (in tonnage). It includes general cargo facilities in West Baton Rouge Parish and a series of marine facilities ranging from north of the capital city to Donaldsonville, from river mile 253 to 168. The nation's farthest-inland deep-water seaport (230 river miles to the Gulf of Mexico), the Port of Greater Baton Rouge handles a large variety of petrochemical products, pulp and paper, grain, molasses, bulk ores, and general cargo.

82

PETROCHEMICAL COMPLEX

Extending between Southern University and downtown Baton Rouge are a number of petrochemical plants. In the foreground, north of U.S. Highway 190, which leads to the Huey Long Bridge over the Mississippi, is the Rhone-Poulenc Basic Chemical Company plant. Across U.S. 190 is the Baton Rouge plant of LaRoche Chemicals, Inc., originally an aluminum plant built during World War II. Reaching southward toward downtown are the Copolymer Rubber and Chemical Corporation, Ethyl Corporation, Formosa Plastics, and Exxon Chemicals plants and the Exxon oil refinery (originally Standard Oil).

PART II
THE ENVIRONS

THE DIVERSION CANAL AND BLIND RIVER

Southwest of Hammond, the Amite River diversion canal draws away excess water (muddy from spring rains in this view) from the Amite River, which drains an area extending as far as Mississippi, north and east of Baton Rouge.

The diversion canal joins Blind River, which, originating near Gramercy, close to the Mississippi River, flows north and eastward into Lake Maurepas. It is one of the best water-skiing and boating areas in the state because, being relatively remote from highway connections, Blind River is still close to its natural state of two hundred years ago.

JEFFERSON COLLEGE

Built in 1838 for the education of sons of Catholic plantation owners, Jefferson College was used as a barracks by Union troops from 1862 to 1864. The facility is now Manresa Retreat House, a Jesuit retreat center for men from southeast Louisiana. Looking toward the banks of the Mississippi River (where the college had its own steamboat landing), the brick-columned main building has two stories plus an attic. Upstairs and down, dormitory rooms line both sides of a hallway extending the length of the building. The Gothic Revival chapel is featured in the foreground.

OAK ALLEY *right*

The major backer of Jefferson College was Valcour Aime, a wealthy antebellum planter known as the Midas of Louisiana. His plantation home burned years ago, but the Greek Revival home of his brother-in-law, Jacques Telesphore Roman, still stands at the end of a magnificent avenue of oaks a hundred years older than the house.

Oak Alley, originally called Bon Séjour, was built between 1837 and 1839. The cathedral-like space beneath the oaks extends the length of three football fields between the house and the levee. The view of the house framed by its alley of oaks is breathtaking.

CRAWFISH SEASON IN THE ATCHAFALAYA SWAMP *left*

One of south Louisiana's industries is the production and processing of crawfish (one never says "crayfish" in south Louisiana). During the spring, which is high-water season, scores of Cajun boatmen tend their traps in the Atchafalaya Swamp, bringing out thousands of pounds of the succulent shellfish.

Living in the swamp was at one time a way of life for many Cajuns, who, expelled by the British in the 1750s from their native Acadia (renamed Nova Scotia, "New Scotland"), found a home along the rivers and bayous of south Louisiana.

CRAWFISH FARMING

In the 1970s and 1980s, crawfish farming became a larger factor in south Louisiana's economy. Now crawfish are raised not only for the local market but also for export around the world.

PETROCHEMICAL PLANTS ON THE MISSISSIPPI RIVER

Sparking a generation-long construction boom between Baton Rouge and New Orleans, large numbers of petrochemical plants began to replace sugarcane fields along River Road in the late 1950s. In this view looking southeast (downriver) below Saint Gabriel, Louisiana, the Mississippi River makes a long, looping bend to form Point Clair, which extends westward toward White Castle (out of the picture at the right).

In the foreground are the river and the Ciba-Geigy plant. Other plants in the background include Cos-Mar, Arcadian, Shell Chemical, and BASF-Wyandotte.

NOTTOWAY

Just upriver from White Castle, on the Mississippi River's west bank, is Nottoway plantation house, built in 1859 for John Hampden Randolph. Originally from Virginia, Randolph's family moved in the early 1820s to Woodville, Mississippi, north of Baton Rouge. In 1841, Randolph relocated to Iberville Parish and built a sugar empire. He retained New Orleans architect Henry Howard in 1859 to design what is considered the largest plantation house in the South still standing. Nottoway's original slate roof covers more than 53,000 square feet. The 3-story mansion has 64 rooms and 200 windows; its architecture is a mixture of Greek Revival and Italianate styles.

BAYOU PLAQUEMINE *left*

On the west bank of the Mississippi River, above White Castle, is Plaquemine, Louisiana, the historic gateway to the Atchafalaya Swamp. Named for Bayou Plaquemine (extending westward from the river toward the top of this picture), the town was a major sawmill center around the turn of the century, processing thousands of board feet of cypress from the Atchafalaya Swamp. In 1909, locks with the highest lift in the world at that time were built to control the flow of water into the bayou. The locks were closed permanently in 1961 and replaced by the larger Port Allen lock. Now the site is a park, commemorating the theme of early river traffic.

DOW CHEMICAL USA

Construction began on the facility for the Louisiana division of Dow Chemical USA in the late 1950s. Now one of the Baton Rouge area's largest employers, Dow occupies the site of Union and several other plantations, a property of over 2,000 acres. The restored Union house and grounds are now an employee recreational facility and conference center for the Louisiana division.

BROWN CHAPEL BAPTIST CHURCH

Although mechanization and the move to the cities have considerably reduced the size of the farming population, there still remain a number of small rural churches that serve the communities with roots on Louisiana's great sugar plantations. Two of the larger plantations in west Baton Rouge were Allendale and Calumet. Holding services twice a month on Calumet Road, adjacent to the plantation of the same name, is Brown Chapel Baptist Church.

STATE CAPITOL DRAGWAY

On U.S. Highway 190 at Erwinville, west of Baton Rouge, is the State Capitol Dragway. In May of each year, the dragway hosts the Cajun Nationals, shown here. The event regularly draws high-performance cars from across the country and more than 50,000 spectators, as dragsters cover a quarter of a mile from a standing start in less than six seconds, with top speeds of over 250 miles per hour.

OLD RIVER CONTROL STRUCTURE

In the northern part of Pointe Coupée Parish is Old River, which connects the southern end of the Red River with the Mississippi River. Where the brown waters of the Mississippi meet the rust-red currents of the Red, the Atchafalaya River is born. From that point to the Gulf of Mexico, it is 155 miles by way of the Atchafalaya, but 325 miles along the Mississippi past Baton Rouge and New Orleans.

Since Capt. Henry Shreve unplugged a giant log raft at the head of the Atchafalaya in 1840, the short, deep river has taken progressively more water from the Mississippi. By the 1950s, it was diverting one-third of the water from the Mississippi, and there was an increasing possibility that the great river would change its course.

The United States Corps of Engineers completed a low-sill and a high-sill structure on Old River in the early 1960s and added another unit (shown here) in the late 1980s. As a result, the Mississippi continues to flow "unvexed to the Gulf."

Sailing on False River

AFTON VILLA GARDENS

Completed in 1849, Afton Villa, a forty-room,
Gothic Revival manor house, burned in 1964,
but its winding avenue of oaks remains, leading to the carefully tended gardens. The lady
of the house was known for her sweet rendi-
tion of the ballad "Flow Gently, Sweet Afton,"
which gave the mansion its name.

ROSEDOWN

One of the most outstanding plantation homes in the South, Rosedown was built in 1835 for Martha and Daniel Turnbull. Rosedown is famous not only for its immaculately restored interior furnishings but also for its expansive gardens, planted under Mrs. Turnbull's direction. She was inspired by the seventeenth-century gardens of Italy and France, which she and her husband had seen in their extensive travels in Europe prior to the Civil War.

After the war, the great cotton plantation underwent a long period of economic decline, which lasted until Catherine and Milton Underwood, of Houston, bought the house and its 2,100 acres in 1955. The Underwoods embarked upon a meticulous eight-year restoration of the house, gardens, and outbuildings.

Featured in countless publications, Rosedown is one of the premier plantations of the South.

Pond and Azaleas at Oakley

OAKLEY

Now the centerpiece of a 100-acre state park south of Saint Francisville, the carefully restored Oakley plantation house was home to John James Audubon while he painted birds of the Felicianas and taught drawing to Eliza Pirrie. The plantation was owned at that time by Mr. and Mrs. James Pirrie, Eliza's parents. Audubon completed thirty-two paintings during his four-month stay at Oakley.

This two-story house, built in 1799, features a raised basement, and its architecture exhibits a Carolina influence.

RIVER BEND NUCLEAR PLANT

Near the Mississippi River, south of Saint Francisville, is the River Bend nuclear plant of Gulf States Utilities, which serves the Baton Rouge area. Across the river, to the west, is the Big Cajun coal-fueled generating plant, owned by Louisiana's electrical co-operatives.

ASPHODEL

South of Jackson is one of the jewels of the Felicianas, Asphodel, built between 1820 and 1830. The delicately scaled Greek Revival plantation home was named by its first owner, Benjamin Kendrick, who drew upon a passage from Homer's *Odyssey* describing an "Asphodel meadow . . . in the fields of Elysium." Asphodel was renovated and restored in the 1950s.

MILBANK

The original seat of Feliciana Parish was Jackson, Louisiana. It is located about halfway between Clinton and Saint Francisville, which became the seats of government of East Feliciana and West Feliciana parishes, respectively, after the division of Feliciana Parish in the 1820s.

Milbank, located in downtown Jackson, was built in 1836 and was the town's first bank. It has served subsequently as a hotel, a private residence, a boardinghouse, a dance hall, and an apothecary. A Union barracks after the fall of Port Hudson in July, 1863, Milbank is currently a bed-and-breakfast inn, restored and authentically furnished as a classic antebellum southern mansion.

BATTLE OF JACKSON CROSSROADS

Port Hudson, twelve miles from Jackson, was the western terminus of the Clinton–Port Hudson Railroad, which connected with Jackson via a spur line, built prior to the Civil War. In May and June of 1863, during the Port Hudson campaign, several clashes took place in the Jackson area, including the Battle of Jackson Crossroads. The event is now re-enacted annually on the first weekend in March.

GLENCOE

North of Jackson, on Louisiana Highway 68, is
Glencoe, one of the largest Queen Anne coun-
tryhouses in the state. Originally built in 1897
for Robert Thompson, Sr., the house burned
to the ground the following year. Thompson
had the house rebuilt exactly as it was, with
one exception: he had it covered with "silver
dollars"—galvanized shingles—for his wife.
Glencoe is now a country inn.

EAST FELICIANA PARISH COURTHOUSE

With a classic Doric colonnade on all four sides, the parish courthouse at Clinton is one of the finest examples of Greek Revival architecture in the South. Built in 1841, the courthouse has been featured in a number of motion pictures, including *The Long Hot Summer*, starring Joanne Woodward and Paul Newman.

LAWYERS' ROW *below*

Predating the East Feliciana Parish courthouse in Clinton is Lawyers' Row, on which construction began in 1825. The last of the five buildings was completed in 1865, near the end of the Civil War. The row reflects the development of Greek Revival architecture in the South, beginning with a brick-columned Doric office, second from the right, and ending with a rougher Doric building at the far right, completed under a wartime economy.

LINWOOD

In 1848, Albert Galatin Carter built an imposing frame plantation home, with massive Tuscan galleries at the front and the rear, on land granted to his father by the Spanish in the 1790s.

During the Civil War, Sarah Morgan Dawson, a resident of Baton Rouge, stayed at Linwood until the surrender of the Confederate garrison at nearby Port Hudson. She later wrote an eyewitness account of the campaign, published as *A Confederate Girl's Diary*, which became a postwar best seller.

PORT HUDSON BATTLEFIELD

While Gen. Ulysses S. Grant and Gen. William Tecumseh Sherman were engaged in the Vicksburg, Mississippi, campaign to close the Mississippi River to the Confederacy, Gen. Nathaniel P. Banks was besieging a much smaller Rebel garrison at Port Hudson, north of Baton Rouge. The bitterly fought campaign began May 22, 1863, and during the almost two-month-long battle, about 6,000 Rebel troops held off nearly 40,000 bluecoats. On Thursday, July 9, the starving defenders surrendered after learning of the fall of Vicksburg on July 4. Union casualties were high, over 5,000, with many men buried where they fell, on ground later to become a national cemetery (foreground). With the fall of Vicksburg and of Port Hudson, the Confederacy was cut nearly in half.

In the background is Georgia-Pacific's Port Hudson paper mill. Many shell fragments, minié balls, and other remnants of the Port Hudson campaign were unearthed during mill construction in the 1960s.

DRILLING IN THE TUSCALOOSA TREND

A drilling rig in the Port Hudson area, north of Baton Rouge, explores for pockets of high-pressure natural gas in the Tuscaloosa Trend, about 17,000 feet below ground level. Pressures in the Tuscaloosa Trend (so-named for its sand and clay, similar to that found just beneath the topsoil in a city in Alabama) can measure over 7,500 pounds per square inch.

PART III
LEISURE AND ENTERTAINMENT

GREATER BATON ROUGE ZOO

Opened in 1970, the 140-acre Greater Baton Rouge Zoo is operated by the East Baton Rouge Parish Recreation and Park Commission. It features approximately 1,000 animals and birds from around the world and employs a staff of 40. The zoo is accredited by the American Association of Zoological Parks and Aquariums and maintains a nationally recognized program of breeding exotic animals.

Among the zoo's most popular attractions are a retired LSU mascot, Mike the Tiger IV, and the largest African antelope collection, including 6 endangered species, of any medium-sized zoo in the United States.

The Mikado, *Performed by the Gilbert and Sullivan Society*

The Baton Rouge Symphony, Performing at the Centroplex Theater

PERFORMING ARTS

The Nutcracker, *Presented by the Baton Rouge Ballet Theatre*

Well-supported by the Baton Rouge community, local performing arts companies that show a high level of professionalism include the Baton Rouge Symphony, the Baton Rouge Little Theater, the Baton Rouge Ballet Theatre, the Baton Rouge Opera/LSU Opera Theater, and the Gilbert and Sullivan Society.

The Baton Rouge Opera/LSU Opera Theater's Production of La Traviata

The Baton Rouge Little Theater's Production of The Music Man

TABBY'S BLUES BOX AND HERITAGE HALL

Authentic blues music can be heard year-round at Tabby's Blues Box and Heritage Hall on North Boulevard. Tabby Thomas, a nationally known musician and performer, decided in the late 1970s to make his home in Baton Rouge, and he opened the nightclub in 1980.

GREAT RIVER ROAD RUN

Sponsored by the Baton Rouge *State-Times* and *Morning Advocate* newspapers, the Great River Road Run comprises a ten-kilometer run and wheelchair race and a one-mile Fun Run/Walk. The event, held the first or second Saturday in April, attracts more than 5,000 participants each year.

SOUTH LOUISIANA CUISINE

No book on Baton Rouge would be complete without mention of the unique cuisine it shares with the rest of south Louisiana. The area is best known for its seafood, prepared with a Cajun flair. South Louisiana feasts often include boiled crawfish, oysters on the half shell, seafood gumbo, hush puppies, charcoal-broiled fish, crawfish étouffé, and other delicacies, such as fried crawfish salad, frog legs, stuffed shrimp, crab balls, fried shrimp, oysters, catfish, and soft-shelled crab.

In one of the best-attended charity events of the year, the Cancer Society of Greater Baton Rouge assembles many of the most accom-

plished chefs and caterers along this section of the Mississippi River for its annual Capital Chefs' Showcase. Proceeds help the society assist over 2,000 individuals a year.

127

JAMBALAYA FESTIVAL *left*

One of the best-known Cajun dishes is jambalaya, a savory mixture of rice, onions, green onions, garlic, bell peppers, and meat or seafood (shrimp, crawfish, chicken, wild game, or sausage, according to the fancy of the cook), all seasoned to taste with a generous dollop of Tabasco sauce.

Jambalaya cooks from the area gather annually in June in Gonzales or Sorrento, below Baton Rouge, for a cook-off in the Jambalaya Festival.

MARDI GRAS

Baton Rouge and surrounding communities (such as New Roads, shown above) celebrate the carnival season with parades. A number of "krewes" hold annual balls. Festivities begin after the religious feast day of the Epiphany and continue for several weeks, culminating in Mardi Gras (Fat Tuesday), the day before the Lenten season begins.

Thirty-First Annual Ball of Baton Rouge's Krewe of Iduna

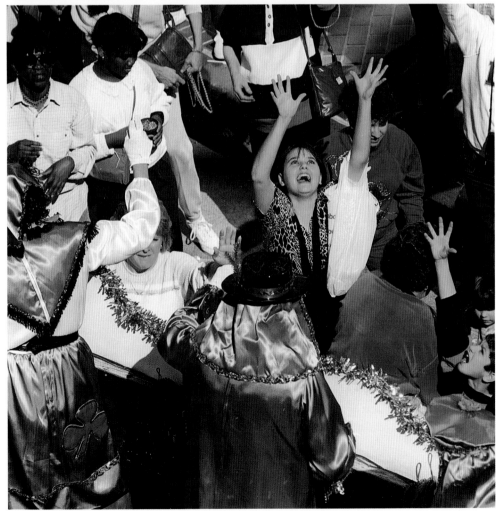

Krewe of Mystique's Mardi Gras Parade in Downtown Baton Rouge

The Spanish Town Mardi Gras parade is known for its unique floats and marching brigades.

CHINESE NEW YEAR

Members of Baton Rouge's Chinese community celebrate the arrival of their new year with lion dances, martial arts demonstrations, lots of firecrackers, and new year's feasts at local Chinese restaurants.

FESTFORALL

Held in May of each year, the capital city's premier arts festival features a children's pavilion, a food fair, a sand sculpture contest, art exhibitions, and a wide variety of musical performances in downtown Baton Rouge near the Old State Capitol.

GREATER BATON ROUGE
STATE FAIR

Each fall, from the last weekend in October
through the first weekend in November, the
Greater Baton Rouge State Fair draws more
than 100,000 to a quarter-mile-long midway
on fairgrounds flanking Bayou Manchac and
Airline Highway (U.S. 61).

BALLOON CHAMPIONSHIP

The Baton Rouge fairgrounds, on the southern border of East Baton Rouge Parish, was the site of the 1989, 1990, and 1991 United States National Hot Air Balloon Championship, which drew over 150 contestants and a large number of spectators each year. The traditional first event, shown here, was an early-morning mass lift-off.

Southern University Basketball

140

LSU Baseball at Alex Box Stadium

Tailgate Parties at the LSU Tiger Stadium

LSU Football

CABINS AT POPLAR GROVE PLANTATION

Although the sugarhouse at Poplar Grove has long been shut down, many of the nearby tenant houses are still occupied, standing in a double row near the Mississippi River just north of Port Allen. Some of the cabins have housed the same families for more than fifty years.

In December, 1990, the Foundation for Historical Louisiana and the West Baton Rouge Development Corporation (with the co-operation of Premier Bank, the landowner) outlined the cabins and much of the sugarhouse with thousands of white lights. A nominal admission fee was charged to view the display, with the proceeds directed toward a Poplar Grove preservation fund. This was the first step in an effort to preserve at least one of south Louisiana's rapidly vanishing plantation villages.

CHRISTMAS AT THE CAPITOL

In December, 1990, as a tribute to the American troops stationed in the Persian Gulf, the grounds of the State Capitol were lavishly ornamented with one and a half million Christmas lights furnished by restaurant entrepreneur Al Copeland. The spectacle was conceived and implemented (with the help of scores of volunteers and Copeland's employees) by the Louisiana Department of Agriculture and Forestry under the direction of its commissioner, Bob Odom.

INDEX